The Wary Politician

Uniting Nations

MC Lunch

" Accountability is the bedrock of good governance "

~ Unknown

Table of Contents

Dedication

Dedicated to all husbands and wives who continue to stand behind their spouses selflessly, despite calls to destroy their families in the name of individual so-called happiness, which often destroys families and society in general.

For their selfless nurturing of marriage, family, children and society under God and all that is good.

The world salutes you.

Preface

This Book is the 3rd in a 3 part Series .
Following Bheki's rise to office, as a regular citizen
from mere observer, to office of Mayor and then
Governor of his province in the country of Mazania,
we follow him on his journey, watch how he manages
to produce success amidst sceptical opposition as
governor.

Later on, after a few years in office he longed for a
quiet life and retires from standing for a second term
only to become a sought after Presidential candidate
by his peers and the electorate that expresses its
longing for his results based approach once more.

Once more he reluctantly agrees to stand for National
elections for a small party, only to have a huge upset
in the elections resulting in his party winning the
presidency.   In this final part of the series we
accompany him from party politics into cabinet and
the battles he faces in effecting numerous changes
that go again the established government norms, as
he challenges the status quo with his no- nonsense
approach amidst tensions at home and the impact
this has on his family, country, region and the United
Nations.

Chapter 1:

Experience & Track Record

On assuming office, Bheki spent some time picking potential future ministers in office with a record of delivery from his own party.   These were mostly to be ministers who had held office in various States or municipalities with a proven track record.   He had learnt over time that his success or lack thereof would be determined to a large extent as a result of the ministers he would surround himself with as President.

To some degree, he and the whole country had known of the previous governments tendency to pick friends, cronies and party influencers who had the gift of the gab but had terrible track records when it came to delivery.

Identifying Suitable Department Heads :
He then went about identifying other potential leaders who had either shown themselves to be sincere in their delivery with preference being given to leaders who had ;

- No Criminal convictions
- Had No pending criminal charges against them

- With those who had produced a firm proposal on how they would deliver if given a chance
- As a last criteria he went about perusing various possible leader's qualifications and other experience that could be used in his soon to be finalised cabinet.

The biggest challenge was that his party had never been in National Government before but had been limited to running municipalities or at best provincial or State Governments as he himself had done prior to the national elections.

<u>First Task for potential Ministers;</u>

Prior to announcing his ministers he gave those in the shortlisted pool a task to to write a one on :

A. Identifying their top 3 priorities if appointed,
B. Identifying top 3 Senior Managers they believed could help them achieve the 3 priorities they had identified.
C. Qualification criteria they would use to pick the candidates

This one page Essay they had to compose in a two hour meeting they would have no chance to prepare for :

Once the 1 page Essay was completed they would be given 10 minutes each to present the Essay.

Performance Agreements & Consequences !

Working closely with his now presidential adviser, Loki, He proceeded to scour the latest and best techniques for tracking performance from both the best performing government and industry.

Loki, proposed a simple five point performance measure to be adopted with the future cabinet to measure effectiveness of agreed objectives, these measures were made up of the following :

- **Financial Performance**
- **Service delivery**
- **Skill Retention and Transfer**
- **Impact on the Economy**
- **Native small business & Employment index**

1. Financial Performance

This element would measure Budget allocation and utilisation, designed to reduce wasteful expenditure and to avoid qualified audits, which often were linked to fraudulent expenditure, also key would be tracking of the ROI (Return On Investment) over an agreed reasonable period.

2. Service delivery

This measure was designed to see how efficient a department was performing compared to other departments bench-marked against an average of the best performing departments in economies of a similar size.

3. Skill Retention and Transfer

In order to reduce the percentage of graduates annually lost to private industry or other governments notably those in Europe.   Also, compulsory shadowing of the most experienced was to be established and contractually made to be track-able using proven industry best practice and incentive.

4. Impact on the Economy:

This would be the measure of how each department contributed to the country's economy overall.   This measure had been the single most important promise to the country from the electioneering slogan of " *Its-the-economy-stupid* " campaign.   In addition Bheki wanted to make sure this cabinet would report on it.

5. Native small business & Employment index .

Given that employment was a massive problem, it had been agreed by experts that most of the jobs in the country that could be performed by unskilled or semi-skilled citizens.   This would be an attempt to manage and curb the uncontrolled entry of so called " *rare skills* " of people from all over the world that business had often used as an excuse not to pay fair wages to locals.

Given that most economies grew when Small & Medium Enterprises(SME) were encouraged and supported, preference to native owned and run SME's would be supported in both formal and the informal sectors alike.   With a key measure being the number of days taken to pay for services rendered by SME's to government departments and private sector alike.   This was an attempt to reduce the notoriously burdensome practice on SME's.

Non Performance & Consequences.
A standard performance agreement would need to be signed by all ministers and each department's management as well as all public servants before they could commence their jobs or office.

Non performance over an agreed time was to be clearly defined with consequences mentioned.   This would serve to reduce the culture of entitlement and partisan loyalty that had ruined the sense of delivery of most of the national public servants.   This would be done with Unions were these existed.   Similarly, unions would be held accountable for not honoring their own agreements.

Chapter 2:

The Cabinet & the Party Executive

Once he had identified each of the department ministers, he would need for his cabinet, to set about identifying the strengths and weaknesses of each ministers.   This would lead to a type of 360 degree evaluation mechanism.

He worked with his confidant, now a presidential advisor, Loki to draw up each department's head strength and weaknesses.   Loki who had been running their company largely by herself for the last few years, had learnt to read people very well and had successfully managed to increase productivity of their Engineering company as Bheki had been consumed by his life in politics.

Up to this point Bheki had taken no direct instruction from the National Party Executive (NPE) with regard to appointments but at the back of his mind he was aware that it would be a matter of time before he would have to discuss his potential *" dream team "* with them or at least with his soon to be Deputy President.

As they reviewed the work done so far with Loki, they had begun to feel comfortable that the criteria was in line with what had helped Bheki to be a successful mayor and later as state governor.

They had learnt a lot over the six years or so since that day they had attended that community meeting in their small town that had catapulted them into a rather unlikely position of being in the country's elevated Government Office.

The preceding year of travel on their holidays in a few progressive countries in Africa and elsewhere, they had come across experiences that helped to have their eyes opened and had made them realise that the were a number of success stories in the continent that they themselves could learn from.

Chapter 3:

The Summon

It had been a long week, first, Bheki was adapting to the whole shock of becoming the country's leading citizen and had asked for a week's leave from the National Party Council (NPC) to get into terms with what had just happened.

He was now faced not only with challenges of having to leave his home and move to the country's capital, to occupy the presidential home, office and other responsibilities as well as his life.

He was slowly getting used to the idea of uprooting Loki, Zina, their young daughter and Langa's life from their accustomed relatively low key existence, to that of being the First family, so to speak.

Although he had thought about it earlier, but now that he had handpicked a few key members of his party to make up his dream team, only now it had dawned on him the changes that would hit his family and change their   life in a way he had never really even dreamt of.

Loki also, in her way was coming into terms with the changes, even though she had put a brave face on things.   In her heart of hearts she realised that she and her family would lose even further what little privacy they had managed to eek out as the Governor or Premier's family.   A concern for their youngest daughter, Zina who was a very shy personality.

This change was even more surprising as more international messages from neighbouring states, from most if not all countries continued to pour in. Only then they had begun to realise how well known they had become.

Loki was worried about being able to cope, but at the same time she was more concerned for her reluctant and weary husband and daughter, who were introverts at heart.

She was worried if it would turn out to be too much for them and what impact or strain in their relationship and family this would bring.   Since they had a month before the official inauguration, she tried to broach the subject of the changes with Bheki, Langa and Zina, one beautiful morning.

" *Bheks…*", she began at the breakfast table early on a Saturday morning.   " *Do you realise I received a message from the Queen this morning ?* "

" *What Queen ?...*", Bheki retorted as he chewed his muesli with one of his eyes glued to the newspaper next to him.

" *T h e Queen !!* " she screamed in disbelief.

" *Mom you mean Queen Elizabeth ?*" Zina curiously added her own question, as her Mom waited with a surprised look on her face.

" *Oh, I received one from the Zulu King yesterday ..* " Bheki added almost without thinking while starring at the newspaper next to him.

" *The Queen of England , Bheks ...!!* " Loki added, in a state of disbelief.

" Queen of *England ?, she 's not my Queen* ", Bheki quipped as he continued chewing his food without even looking at Loki.

The Mother, daughter and Son, looked at each other with their mouths half open as they shook their heads in disbelief.

Before, Loki could retort to the rather unexpected response, the house phone rang and Langa sprinted to pick it up, he was expecting a call from a friend and had thought the ringing phone was for him.

" *Hello, …., howzit Bro ?* ", he asked, not realising he was on speaker phone.

" Hello, is your Dad home " the serious female voice responded, from the other side . It was Ms. Zungu, the Mazania party President.

Recognising her rather unique Swati accent, Bheki arose and walked to the phone, picked up the phone and put the speaker-phone off, not wanting their children to hear whatever it was Ms. Zungu had phoned about.

" *Morning Bheki, I trust you are well ?*" she continued.

" *I am very sorry to phone you so early, but we need you to come in tomorrow, we have some important issues we need to discuss with the National executive .*"

" *Tomorrow ?, I've already made plans, that's too soon, can't it wait till Friday ?,* "

" *Well, it will have to , but just be aware that the executive team is very concerned and unhappy with the individual meetings you've been having with some of the senior members of the party* "

Realising Loki, Zina and Langa were probably listening to the conversation, he thanked Ms. Zungu and asked if he could call her back later in the day. Once agreed he hung up the phone and returned to finish his breakfast .

.

Loki, sensing and observing Bheki's demeanor realised something was amiss as the love of her life looked a little tense, but resolved to discuss with him later after the teenagers had left for their Saturday classes.

Chapter 4:

Agreed Conditions for Candidacy Acceptance

Bheki had already resigned his position as premier and was intent on leaving politics when his party had pleaded with him to be their national presidential candidate, this had become necessary given his popularity with the voters and the short time they had left before election day.

Prior to Bheki's acceptance as the party's Presidential candidate, he had put forward the following conditions.

1st Condition: **He would serve only for one term.**

Prior to agreeing to being the Face of the party just before the national elections that saw Bheki's party win the Presidential vote, he had given the National Mazania Leadership executive a number of key conditions prior to agreeing to be the Presidential candidate, this he had done after days of serious soul searching.

One of these was that he would serve for only one five year term as the party's parliamentary leader, this meant for a maximum of 5 years, He had put forward these conditions after serious reflection as he was reluctant even then to stay in politics.   This had been his way to meet his earlier decision and commitment to leave politics.

In so doing he effectively agreed to be deputy president of the party, with Ms. Zungu remaining the party's president.   Effectively this agreement had not displaced any executive member since he had effectively taken Mr.Goto's position who had defected to a rival party.   For this reason the existing party executives were happy to have a strong popular candidate that was no seen as a competitor for any of their positions.

He argued that during this 5 year term , his shadow cabinet would need to reach agreement with regard to his vision that he had outlined to the party leadership, to which they subsequently agreed to.

2nd Condition : Reduction of Public Official's perks.

If the party won the elections, which seemed unlikely at the time of these condition being accepted by the executive, they were the third largest party and not even the official opposition.   The condition stated that ministers, including cabinet ministers would have no more than two official vehicles each as part of the executive fleet, as opposed to the five and often more vehicles which were being used by Members of Parliament and senior Government Officials.

Bheki had viewed this as an unnecessary expenditure that flaunted public funds in a country with a high unemployment and struggling economy and wanted to change public expenditure perceptions to become more frugal and reflect the country's true economy.

In addition to this no Luxurious and expensive Brands of vehicles would be bought or leased but only non-luxurious brands from a minimum of at least three manufacturers, with priority given to locally manufactured vehicles and services.   This would be done in an effort to boost the local manufacturing industries and therefore , job creation (exceptions would only be permitted after good motivation and approval by parliament, if at all).

3rd Condition: **Prioritised use of Government Services by all State Employees.**

All party officials from top ministers to the most junior clerk employed by the government, would be obliged to use Public Services and not private Services for their healthcare, education and whenever possible they would use State owned services for themselves.

This would include Water, Electricity ,Health, Flights , Telecommunication, State owned Conference and Hotel facilities, etc.

This Condition Bheki had put down after mounting citizen's complaints on how state run entities often provided shabby or poor services while elected officials and public servants were often seen running to private owned business when the ones they were overseeing or in charge of were left to wallow in inefficient delivery of services.

In his heart, he had written this down after witnessing some of the positive provision of services by some governments such as the National Health Service (NHS) in the UK, transport services in most of the so called first world countries and could not understand why in his home country the same politicians could get away with providing less than stellar services themselves and the voters that put them into office in the first place.

<u>4th Condition:</u> **Ability to appoint or dismiss**
advisors unilaterally.

Bheki would want to have a full say around the team
in his office who would work with him.

In the end the party executives had officially accepted
the conditions Bheki had put forward, even though
the were some reservations in their minds about
them.

They had eventually agreed largely because they had
no choice and not for any other reason.

Chapter 5:

The Party Executive's Challenge

The Party's vs. Country's Priorities

Finally, Friday arrived, Bheki had flown early that morning to arrive early for the 9am meeting at the party's head office.   It had been a difficult flight for him since now as President elect, he received more attention from all who saw him as everyone wanted to congratulate him.   Often people wanted to congratulate and take a Selfie him, his security team had their hands full at times.

From the time when he entered the airport terminal, as well as passengers on his flight as well as when arriving at the party head office, well wishers wanted to speak to him.   This had been more attention than ever before and he had gently smiled and greeted as many as he could by waving to them.

As he entered the Mazania Party's main conference room, he was greeted kindly by the receptionist and Ms.Zungu, however most of the other national executive members had a cold air about them, even though they appeared friendly enough.

After some formalities and a light working breakfast
with other members, the meeting began.

Opening the Meeting, Ms. Zungu welcomed him to
his first official national executive meeting as a
member since in the last meeting he had attended
merely as a guest of honor ,today he was attending
as the deputy President elect of the party and
Parliamentary President elect.

The Agenda was brief, they would discuss the
positive outcome and performance of the party to
date and its first ever win of the Presidential office.
They were now to prepare for the national
presidential inauguration in about a month's time.

Ms.Zungu, having welcomed everyone, made it
known that the main agenda item for discussion was
the composition of the country's national executive or
cabinet as its popularly known.

Before she could completely introduce the main topic
of principles that should guide the identification and
composition of the cabinet, a Mr.Tutu, raised his
hand and once Ms. Zungu who was chairing the
meeting had finished her opening remarks, she gave
Mr. Tutu the opportunity to speak.

Mr. Tutu, who was the party's Treasurer, remarked: "
We hear that our President-elect here, has already

selected his cabinet ? ", he asked with a sarcastic tone in his voice and a self-righteous smirk on his face.   The air of tension in the room could be cut with a knife as all the eyes turned to look at Bheki who was seated two seats away from Ms. Zungu, next to the party's secretary.

Mrs. Zungu, feeling a little uneasy but reading the burning same question in everybody's expression retorted. " *Mr. Tutu, thank you for your question, but Bheki I have to ask* " as she paused to take a deep breath, then she asked " *Is this true ?* "

Bheki taking a sip of water , then began his response " *Ms. Zungu, you will recall that as part of my agreement to stand as our national party candidate I put forward some conditions that this very same national executive reviewed and finally agreed to, those conditions are as per the minutes you were kind to copy me on, I have them here* ", Bheki concluded as he lifted the transparent folder with the minutes .

Silence followed as Bheki paused and waved the minutes with his hand raised up high, as a way of driving his point.   Before he could continue, Mr. Tutu interrupted once more …" *Surely you can't hold us to that , we never really expected to win the Presidency that's why we agreed to that* ", he concluded.   Some

mumbling amongst the attendees could be heard,
then Bheki continued .

" *Madam Chair, am I to understand that this national
executive's word and resolution of the meeting held
in its last session, which discussed and approved my
conditions for acceptance of my national candidacy
was a lie ? "*

Before, the Chairperson Ms.Zungu could respond ,
Mr.Tutu in a scornful manner   responded   " *Yes,
but , but   uh….*"

" *Mr. Tutu ! …*" the Chairperson interrupted him, " *I
am the Chairperson of this meeting, that question is
directed to me* " , the room and Mr. Tutu finally
quietened down.

" *Well, Mr. Deputy Chairperson, Bheki , that's a fair
question you have asked, Yes, this executive board
resolved to accept your conditions as you had put
them forward, so it was not a lie, to give a direct
answer*", then looking at Mr. Tutu sternly said,   "
Right Mr Tutu ? ", nodding sheepishly Mr. Tutu
concerted.

Continuing Ms Zondo added " *Now that we have
cleared that up, let me highlight the general principle
of how executive members are generally elected* "

She proceeded to mention that everyone in the room was there as an outcome of a National Party Conference election process and similarly, the normal process to follow would have to be as a result of the National executive agreement on the candidates who would head the various ministries of the national government.   At the end he asked if the executive members would like to comment or ask questions on this point.

The majority of them agreed with her summary, although a few pointed out that Bheki although elected by a national conference as such, he had clearly received a majority vote of the country and therefore was qualified to be in the executive as well.

Bheki listened carefully and at the end asked to say a few words .   " *Ms. Zungu and fellow members , thank you for your comments.   It is true I had spoken to a number of the candidates and some of you in this room as part of my learning about potential good candidates for possible appointment to various ministries.* "

He proceeded to point out that given that he would be serving for one five year term , he would have a short time to effect any meaningful change, it is for this reason he had been proactive to identify candidates .

Reading the room and noting that some who he had not approached and considered for the cabinet , he added:

" *I had taken the initiative to approach leaders with a proven positive track record of delivery in office, if you must know as to what criteria I used, I interviewed only candidates who had practically worked either in a municipality or provincial government like I did, Why ?, because in five years we will not have a chance to train new senior decision makers with no public office experience, and lastly, ..uhm, If I am not allowed to serve the first term with a cabinet team with a proven track record that I can trust and work with ,I will have to seriously consider stepping aside as president,as I will not go down as another politician who promised one thing and failed ...*"   he concluded , as the room stayed silent for what felt like an eternity.

After a controlled cough and after the point he had just made was slowly sinking-in to all the national executive, Ms.Zungu came to life and asked " Can *you share who you have in mind* "

Bheki getting up, asked If he could write on the Flip-chart that stood next to the main screen.

He proceeded to write on the Board top ministries of Finance, Trade & Industry, Foreign Relations,

Energy, Home Affairs, Transport, Resource and Business.

He then explained his rational for prioritising on these while also listing the relevance to improving the Economy.

When asked to give a list of ministers or leaders of each, he pointed out that the process was ongoing and would be completed in a weeks time, however all they need to do, was to identify likely candidates, was to think of the most senior executives with a proven positive execution experience and those without convictions or imprisonment in the last 5 years.

Putting his pen aside, he then added " *All my political career I have always worked closely with Loki ,my wife, as my advisor that I can trust, I intend to keep her as my official presidential advisor as indicated at the time of my acceptance of the party's national presidential candidate.   Now, does anyone have a problem with that ?..*"

Mr. Nene, gaining an air of confidence, raised his hand and asked, " *Deputy President, won't that be considered to be nepotism ? *"

Bheki smiled, looked at the executive, folded his arms and asked " *Apart from the fact that the is no law against it,   who of you here never talks to their partner at home and share their work with them ? "*

The whole room burst into nervous laughter and all stood up and gave him an applause which went on for some time until Ms. Zungu had to call the room to order and make a last request.

"Mr. Vice President, with the Presidential inauguration taking place in 4 week, can you commit to share with me on behalf of the party executive next week the names of the cabinet ministers you're considering ? "

Bheki taking his seat , nodded and replied " *Absolutely Madam President* "

With all the executive members seemingly satisfied, the meeting was adjourned as they all went to have lunch together and to speak informally amongst themselves.

Before having a drink himself, Bheki asked to have a word with Ms. Zungu in private, to which Ms. Zungu obliged and was able to speak privately with her.

Once they were alone in Ms. Zungu's rather imposing office, Bheki broke the silence. " *Ms. Zungu I have a problem and a proposal* ", he began as Ms. Zungu sipped on her coffee as she sat back into the colourful office chair.

" *Yes, Bheki , of course , what's on your mind ? .*", she inquired. Bheki stood up walked out of the office, closed the door and waited a few seconds and re-entered before Ms. Zungu understood what strange behaviour this was that Bheki was exhibiting.

As he entered, he again closed the door behind him and with a stern look on his face said in a serious expression-less face " *Ms. Deputy President of Mazania, good afternoon* ".   It took a few moments for the penny to drop in Ms. Zungu, who then responded . " *I'm no deputy president of Mazania ...* " then Bheki continued .

" *There is no better candidate for me to call on, you have held single handedly held this party together long before I was even invited to this building, you have proven yourself and I need a strong deputy to help me keep the party politics and other administrative distractions from me , as you know I need to focus on the economy,...*"

Ms. Zungu who was uncharacteristically stunned and lost for words, tried to speak and quipped " *Uhm, Bheki,   well , no,…...let me think about it   *" she took yet again another long sip of her coffee and continued " *I am not good with public speeches and* debates, I am more of a behind the scenes person …., in case you don't know "

Bheki sensing her hesitation, remarked " *Exactly , but you are good at what you do , for continuity , this party and now this ruling party will need a steady hand to keep the country going when I finish my five years in office. "*

Without waiting for a response, Bheki continued " *You have kept your head , have been fair and honestly , I would feel more comfortable with you as my deputy "*

" *So …let me get this straight, you want me to be the country's deputy president while you remain as party deputy President ? "* she finally blurted out her question.

Bheki with a big smirk on his face responded   " *Absolutely* ". Bheki wanted to have this arrangement since he realised he did not want to be distracted by what he considered as petty party politics since he wanted to serve only for one term.

Ms. Zungu had never considered this possibility, but calmly suggested, " *Lets do this, when you inform me next week of your final cabinet minister's names, I'll let you know what I have decided* ", she concluded .

Bheki walked to her, shook her rather nervous hand, and declared "*Great, I must go now if I am not to miss my flight ,I look forward to speaking to you again soon,   Deputy President* ", he said rather mockingly as he put on his jacket , picked up his brief case. Ms. Zungu got up and began to walk her party's President-elect to the foyer where his driver waited for him.

The Cabinet

About two week later, Bheki had finally managed to identify all of the key members of his to be ' dream-team ', surprisingly enough he also picked two incumbent ministers from the then ruling party in the sectors of Education and Health, his logic being he wanted minimal disruption to these two sectors and chose to retain the ministers because of wanting to ensure minimal disruption to the relatively good work that had been done until then.

A number of the ministers he identified turned out to be shadow ministers who had held office in some form before.

Once he had had time time to prepare a presentation explaining the logic behind his ' dream-team ',he made an appointment to present these to the party president Ms. Zungu.

The day of the meeting arrived and he was able to explain his logic for the names he picked insisting that with only 5 years or 1 term in office he wanted to ensure a minimal number of political appointees owing to party politics and affiliation would not do, instead he made it clear that in a year's time, he would consider making changes if non-performance became a problem.

After the meeting, Ms. Zungu informed the rest of executive members sincerely

With the National Executive Team in agreement , consensus was reached with all members and the task of identifying senior administrators or Director Generals of the departments would begin working with the appointees.
Similarly, Ms. Zungu accepted and confirmed her willingness to become the country's deputy president.

The Inauguration promises

The week of the Presidential Inauguration arrived , the party and country worked feverishly to manage the transitional process with incumbent ministers and all relevant preparations were made to ensure a smooth transition.

During his Presidential Inauguration speech, Bheki highlighted his and the party's priority areas in light of the promises they had made during the elections campaign.   Key points in his speech included:

✧   The establishment of a lean and frugal administration, that would see a reduction in the number of lavish vehicles and aeroplane fleet which had until then been enjoyed by cabinet ministers of the latest and some of the most expensive and imported luxury car brands, let alone various services they enjoy, that are paid for by the taxpayer.

✧   A Change in private sector service transition for health, education and other sectors from private service providers to public service providers. Most if not all public servants were extremely unhappy about this particular aspect and a lot of complaints emanated in the media and a host of news and talk shows covered this aspect for the preceding and subsequent months thereafter. After the inauguration, interesting enough the majority of the country's electorate, was elated and spoke positively of this.

One quote that stood out from his speech directed to those employed by government that would ring out onto every news or social media site would be *" If you don't like it - Lets Fix it "*, which again became something of the most memorable part of his inauguration speech and would go on to define his first year in office.

Chapter 6:

The Inauguration Promises

On the day before the inauguration, Bheki and Loki worked together on his speech, the Presidential office had crafted two separate speeches for him. After re-reading them Bheki & Loki could not pick either, they had the feeling that they were both beautifully crafted but were too wordy and too generic for their liking.

After looking at his conditions for acceptance once more Bheki felt that this is what mattered to the people and he chose to focus on the issues he had become aware as to what mattered to his countryman so they could easily understand and hold his administration to account on, he then decided to make these his presidential promises to the electorate as part of his inauguration speech.

As president, one of the first campaigns he embarked on was an educational campaign on how the economy work ran from his now presidential office working closely with the State Communications Department focusing only on how and why the changes were important, highlighting on loyalty to consuming local products and services as compared to consuming imported good and services.

He often insisted that the final measurement be the Number of Jobs saved or created and the Cost benefits derived. His engineering approach of constant measurement shone through as he reduced the amount of political speak that often went over most people, preferring to provide visual charts or graphics to simplify the message.

In, this way measurement and reporting became the new mantra in his administration, just like it had been in his time as Governor and earlier as Mayor.   Long gone were the feel good generic adverts as he insisted that the whole country needed to know and rally behind meeting the targets set for each department.

The Auditor General, working with the deputy president, Ms. Zungu was tasked to lead the measurement and Statistics to be used for the reporting in an effort to ensure accuracy and unjust inflation of numbers.

In Short the Inauguration Presidential promises were similar to the election campaign promises which were centred on the Economy, these were :

A. Departments contribution to the Economy, Jobs and reduction of Public Official's perks.

B. Prioritised Usage of State owned Services (
Education, Health, Transport,Communication,etc.)

C. Performance based appointment and reporting of employees with priority hiring given to natives with a clear plan to address areas of insufficient skills, working with the training Associations.

D. Re-in-statement of national values including compulsory prayer in Schools and public meetings.

Chapter 7:

The Regional Summit

It was shortly after his installation as president that as part of the routine regional meetings, Bheki was informed of a summit that was due to take place in Batswana, a neighbouring country.

He was briefed about the regional priorities and commitments that had been signed by his predecessors as part of the country's role and responsibility.   As part of his preparation he had taken the time to read through the agreed priorities and commitments made on behalf of Mazania.

However he observed that when he was comparing the priority areas a few things were not quantified and the was very little by way of timelines or measures to which they could hold each other to.   Some of these areas included :

- Trade and Economic Infrastructure
Given his focus on improving the economy, he noted that although the was acknowledgement of the legacy of colonial infrastructure which was hampering efficiencies of trade and subsequently their

economies, not much development had been made since independence.   Everyone knew that the colonial train and ports infrastructure was primarily designed to move raw material and other goods to ports for export, but not much had been done for inter-country trade that countries now needed if their economies were to improve.

- Porous Borders & Job Creation
He also noted that often the countries had porous borders that resulted often in undocumented migrants and contraband that usually escaped the taxation and duties that went with regular trade practices.   This in turn contributed to unpaid taxes   and loss to the economy of Mazania.

These porous borders often were the cause of illegal immigrants that unfortunately caused problems in his country.   In cases of contraband and other crimes, from the days as governor he had become aware of cases from earlier years as governor of how often this resulted in exploitation and trafficking of innocent people.

From his national priorities he realised this was one of the factors that would impact his presidential promises about job creation if not addressed.
Little or no mention was made in the inter-country agreements about how these problems were supposed to be addressed.

As part of the regional meetings he attended they had become aware that some of the neighboring states and even across the continent the were some who had been calling for the dissolution or removal of physical country borders.

This was largely based on the argument that most of the Continent's borders had come into existence following the colonisation of most of Africa.   This was perhaps somewhat reflected in most of the predominance of French, Portuguese and English being spoken across most of the continent.

Bheki's personal take on this argument was that in order to improve governance in each country the time was not right for the universal opening of borders as this would most likely result in people moving to countries with better services without the requisite infrastructure and budgets needed to cater for the uncontrolled influx of people.

He conceded, however that over time the opening of borders would make sense, hence his party and him were in agreement that for starters Infrastructure provisioning and economic " opening-up " of borders would be the first aspect of the eventual relaxation of borders in this regard.

He however insisted that each of the governments involved would similarly need to demonstrate acceptable progress in their country with regard to trade and business infrastructure at least on an annual basis.

- Visa

Where Visas were needed for visitors, often these were issued in a non-standard manner often depending on whether the individual coming into their countries was African or not.   This had been due to legacy issues that were unfairly applied and effecting their own citizens.   Again, this had an impact on the economy and migration and sadly often discriminated against their very-own citizens !

- Law Enforcement

Flowing from the issue of porous borders and illegal migration, many issues of law enforcement across the five countries resulted in one form or other.

- Differences in Priorities & Timelines !

One of the biggest concern he noted was that although priority areas had been identified, the was no firm timelines   or action plans, this made the whole ideas of priorities somewhat laughable, he had thought to himself.

- An Effective Peer Review mechanism

From observing previous summit meetings ,he often noted that some of these summits and meeting had become something of a perk for executives who would travel to other countries almost as an opportunity to go shopping and as some form of unofficial holiday at taxpayer's expense.

Although the relations of the executives were generally pleasant and friendly enough, very little of holding each other to task on performance was hard to witness, except once more the lavish expensive hotels, venues and cars, were often the most memorable sights.   As part of his presidential promises this would once more be a bone for him to pick especially when the time came for his country to host a regional meeting !

- Currency and Trade

Given Bheki's belief that the health of the economy was key towards improving the well being of a country and its people, he noted that very often the five countries in his region traded using foreign currencies, typically the dollar.   He found this reality rather strange given that as independent African countries the was no longer good reason as to why they could not use one or more of their currencies. Often this meant that when trading in their own products and services often this practice made them vulnerable to the whims and fluctuations of what happened half way around the planet, let alone interest rate fluctuations set elsewhere.

He shook his head silently as he peered through the window watching his beautiful advisor, Loki who was working in the afternoon sun in their garden. To stretch his legs, he walked outside to speak to her, after giving her a peck on the cheek, he asked, "*So, why do we need to pay for Batswana's diamonds in dollars ? "*.   Loki with a strained expression responded " *What, dollars ?, but why ? "*

He bent down and began to help her pick the strawberries as they discussed the issue in the warm afternoon sun.

The day of the two day summit finally arrived, this was their first trip together as the Presidential couple. Loki had managed to convince her "*Boss* " President not to do anything rash but to use the summit to meet the other leaders and to familiarise himself with how things were done.

They arrived at the sumptuous hotel, were the summit was being held.   The Batswana President proved to be a great host, later in the evening, Loki finally had a chance to meet some of the President's wives and was warmly welcome as talk varied from the services and the luxurious shopping they would be able to do.   Some of the ladies proved to be smart and well informed about the summit as they got to know more about each other, Loki discovered.

One of the ladies joked saying : " *Congratulations, at least you are being recognised as an official advisor, we are not* ", as the other ladies laughed out loud. One of the ladies quipped "*I see him all the time, I surely don't want to be discussing projects and proposals back at home, its hard enough just looking good all the time* " she added as a loud raucous laughter followed from the beautifully clad fairer sex.

On the last day of the Summit, The new Mazanian president had kept reasonably quiet and had not said anything that stood out.   However, as final speeches were being made away from the media and cameras, one of the Presidents, an elderly President of BaSotho, Mr. Motsie , who had been serving his country for well over 15 years, raised his hand and asked a question:

"*My President* " referring to Bheki who had just finished his concluding remarks, "*may I ask a question regarding something you said during your inauguration address* ", without waiting for a response he continued " *I note that you promised to do away with some of the benefits or perks as you put it and now expect government officials to use national hospitals, schools and the like ..., were you really serious about that ?*", he asked with a disapproving tone and blank expression on his face.

Bheki, caught unaware and a bit startled, wondered for a moment why this question was even asked since it was not related to his closing remarks.

The Host President of Batswana, seeing that his guest was somewhat caught by surprise, interjected saying " *Colleagues , lets stick to the agenda , we are all politicians, that's how we manage politics* ", he added with a nervous chuckle.

Bheki having regained his composure, looked at Loki, who instinctively shook her head, almost as saying don't respond to that.   With the five or so *Presidents coyly laughing off the matter Bheki began " Well Mr. President, thank you, you've been a great host , however , the is a need to address the question since its directed at me and it may have an impact on our region overall* ", he said as he paused, and took a sip from the bottled water next to him.

" *Yes, I said those words and I meant them ...*" he responded emphatically, by this time, the sniggering and laughter in the room had ceased.   " As you may be aware, I promised my people that I would serve one 5 year term as I am eager to return to being just a nobody who minds his own business." by now emotional retort had quietened down everyone, and one could hear a pin drop.

" *So, if I am to honour that promise and deliver on the promise I made, as you no doubt heard our campaign slogan Its-the-economy-stupid , then being frugal with our meagre budgets and focusing on the economy its the only way I can see of delivering on that,and Yes, why should we as leaders of our countries be exempt from leading by example, I cannot for the life of me see why each one of us would need more than one or two vehicles at the most of some expensive foreign sourced luxurious vehicles paid for by our poor, unemployed, often struggling electorate.   Mr. President you being more experienced than me in this role..*" said Bheki as he focussed his gaze on the veteran President, before continuing.

"*… perhaps you can tell me if living in luxury at the expense of our taxpayers is a justified way to lead by example, personally I cannot see how.*"

The elderly statement nodded in response to the answer , although feeling a little embarrassed felt the need to defend his earlier question.   " *Well I've increased employment, built schools and other things in my country , I deserve a bit of luxury* ", he concluded.

Bheki not wanting to pursue the matter relented " *You may well have done so, however having listened to all the deliberations over the last two days , I know that our region is performing way below other similar economies with similar populations and resources, I for one don't deserve nor need such a lifestyle, perhaps as a way of managing expectations, when you come to our country, please don't expect a lavish lifestyle* ", Bheki concluded as he left the podium to resume his seat having completed his closing remarks.

The Host president thanked him for his response as the room continued to mutter and comment silently among the presidents and senior officials.

With some of the Presidents feeling uncomfortable and muttering sounds of "self righteous …", the Host president decided to speedily make his closing remarks, thanked everyone and closed the conference and they all broke for Dinner.

During Dinner discussions continued informally amongst the delegates and Bheki continued to state his position clearly without backing down on his commitments but respectfully agreeing to see the others viewpoints and not allowing himself to be intimidated by different views.

Back in the hotel before bedtime Loki shared with
Bheki how some of the women had been offended by
his views and 'self righteous 'manner.

Bheki hearing this turned to his loving advisor and
asked, " and do you agree with them ? ", Loki
knowing that nothing would shake his loving
husband's stubborn view on this, responded by
merely holding his husband and whispered " Never ",
and gently the couple embraced as the light was
turned off.

Chapter 8:

The State of the Nation Address

After some six months in office, it had become time
for the annual State of the Nation Address (SONA).
As part of this process,   Bheki had been very
uncomfortable in the build up and felt that he was ill
prepared, so he chose to focus on reporting on the
key campaign & inauguration promises, this way at
least he knew that the electorate could relate to his
speech.

As part of his preparation working with the National
Cabinet, he received feedback and statistics of some
of the changes that had been effected since his party
took office.   This would include :

✧   The Department's contribution to the Economy
    and reduction of Public Official's perks.

✧   Prioritisation and usage of State owned Services
    (Education,Health,Transport,Communication,etc.)

✧   Updates on Performance based appointment
    and reporting of employees with prioritised   hiring
    given to native Nationals, with a clear plan to

address areas of insufficient skills, working with the training Associations.

✧ Re-instatement of National values including Compulsory Prayer in Schools & Meetings as part of the election campaign promises.

Working with the Auditor General's office and subsequent Statistics of the key departments were compiled with graphs that most of the populations could understand. Twenty four hours before the SONA, each department's vital statistics were released to the country, with most newspapers allocating at least half a page to them in some form.

His Advisors and cabinet ministers were opposed to this move and cautioned against publicising the figures. On this he asked that at least one prime statistic be released as a way of reaching a truce with his cabinet.   When asked which of the statistics, he replied   *"This party campaigned on the economy, so let us share the contribution of each department to the economy   either directly in the form projects contributing to the economy and the number of jobs filled from the many vacancies they may have had. "*

After some heated debate the cabinet relented after he mentioned that after the SONA, he would have a cabinet reshuffle for non performers, as a show of good faith , he agreed to give the poorly performing cabinet ministers, half a year's grace period within which to show improvement.   On hearing this the whole cabinet agreed.   The poorly performing ministerial heads were understandably concerned to be seen in a poor light.

As part of the Press's build up, all the key department's with a few strategic departments exempted, for security reasons, predictably all the major news outlets led with stories comparing the different department's performance.

Opening his SONA speech, after being welcome and introduced by the Speaker of Parliament, along the traditional announcer as was the country's custom, Bheki began his speech.

" *My fellow citizens, guests, Ministers and Mr. Speaker ...*", this opening line turned out to be the opposite of what was the custom and underlined to indicate his prioritisation of the regular proverbial man in the street over the cabinet and members of parliament.   The next day he would be criticised for this but merely answered " *Did the parliament vote for me or did the regular citizen vote for all of us ?* ", which went to silence all his detractors.

With the Press having splashed out the key stats and various media talk-shows had done some analysis of the departmental statistics and critiquing on the economy, he felt he did not have to to into too much details as they had been touched on by the media.

Bheki's speech was unorthodoxically short focusing on the areas of regional trade, borders, education and job creation.   As he attempted to highlight the impact of the key departments, some of the parliamentarians would mention the statistics as he called out each key department :

" *On Health's contribution to the economy…*"
someone blurted out " *15%* "'.   As he mentioned the next department , with some chuckling being heard in the house.

" *On Mining and Resources, contribution to the economy …*" again someone would blurt out   "25% ", with Bheki, smiling quietly.   The speaker of the house called the members to order and so it continued.

Although they interrupted his speech , Bheki smiled about it and chuckled together with half the house and so it continued until all of the key departments had been mentioned, with Bheki, merely re-iterating the percentage with a thumbs-up sign.

At the end he remarked. " *Fellow Citizens, Mr. Speaker , I am very pleased to see that you for the first time don't need me to tell you the impact on the economy by each department* " he began. " *Therefore I trust you will agree that you have begun to see the impact on your life , as indicated by the percentages some of you were shouting out* "

He then continued   "*Although we've have had resistance from most of our executives and senior members of our administration who complained and said that the poor service from government entities was not ideal, we can all now see how earnestly the same executives and senior members of these public entities have begun and continue to make inroads to improving the very entities they are in charge of running.* "   Taking a long pause , he had a sip of water and exclaimed " *this was our first half a year in office, my party and I ,we Thank you.* "

Like a man at the end of a long day's work he resumed his seat with a standing ovation that rung out for some minutes with what seemed an eternity that caused him to come to tears overcome with tears of joy.

With the speaker trying to calm everyone but without success, he finally got up and acknowledged the applause now coming from the same cabinet and opposition benches that had criticised him mercilessly in preceding months.

Perhaps more touching was the sight of the guest president Motsie of BaSotho, a 15 year veteran of a neighbouring state, who had previously been one of his most vehement critics in that first Regional summit he had attended some months earlier, who had questioned Bheki's inauguration promise to do away with lavish perks of expensive foreign cars and expensive lifestyle and hotels and jokingly laughed at his comments claiming that he deserved certain perks.

On this occasion occasion though, the honourable Mr. Motsie who was seated on the executive part of the public gallery, was on his feet and instead of clapping his hand was seen giving a formal salute to Bheki, which in Mr. Motsie's military training was the greatest respect a former soldier could give to another leader.

After bowing in acceptance and similarly offering him a salute albeit from afar the house steadily came to order and the speaker was able to resume and finally conclude the business of the day .

Chapter 9:

Floods, Corruption & Commissions of Enquiry

As part of his first term in office, Bheki, experienced various challenges like any leader in office most likely due to his party's inexperience of running the country. Through it all his relationship with Loki and most of the good cabinet ministers they had picked right from the beginning and grew to become an efficient team. Some of the challenges they would experience in the first year would include :

Torrential Rains and Storms :
Some of the first challenges they experienced, was when the summer rains came.   Freak storms came and a lot of destruction was caused to the country's infrastructure with, dams that were filled to over-capacity with major erosion impacting some of the country's infrastructure including roads, dams and various bridges that were washed away especially in low lying areas.

Working with experts in the agriculture and water management services they managed to pre-empt the most vulnerable areas and worked to minimise harm to the citizens by relocating some, where this became necessary.

Working with the neighboring states the regional countries worked well together to further rescue citizens in water logged rural areas and in so doing further improved relations not just economically but for emergency responses as well between countries.

Corruption :

Later on some investigations into the financial commitments the country had signed for in the sourcing of Locomotives and power infrastructure were found to have been unprocedural.

These had come to light after *The Mazanian*, the local national paper, had uncovered shady dealings that were done during the the previous administration.   Nevertheless as the seating President, Bheki had to deal with a commission of enquiry that had been instituted before his administration had taken office.

One of the major issues was the discovery that Mr.Goto as Chairman of an oversight commission had authorised the purchase of these assets without going through some of the necessary checks and balances from the reserve bank resulting in undue authorisation of the acquisition of these assets.

As President now, Bheki had to now deal with Mr. Goto, his party's former parliamentary leader and his predecessor and others in addressing these issues. These matters in some ways proved to be one of the biggest challenges he had to deal with after assuming the Presidency.

Being the methodical person that he was, he had appointed some of his most trusted officials from his previous roles to deal with them.   In due time he was confident that these matters would be dealt with appropriately but insisted on maintaining verification procedures.

As the saying goes, ' *Trust-But-Verify* ' and in order to ensure adequate progress was made he insisted on having a fortnightly update with the head of the investigation teams whenever possible, or he would ask his deputy, Ms. Zungu to handle the meetings when he was unavailable.

Chapter 10:

Judicial Service Commission Challenges

As if things could only get worse, allegations of undue appointments of some of the country's judiciary, similarly came out, this caused the country to call into question as to how 'just' the judiciary really were.

Given that the Judiciary, remained a key part of the country's democratic establishment, this had brought a lot of distrust of the government and resulted in a lot of citizens and investors alike, questioning the country's reputation and cast doubts on some of sensitive cases going through the courts..

Given that local and global investors alike, as well as sentiment and regard for the country's reputation was key to being able to garner support internationally, let alone receive goodwill and the ever precious investment from foreign direct investment, this aspect had to be dealt with as efficiently as possible.

This development caused him a lot of strain, fortunately he was able to delegate it to Ms.Zungu, his number two, who happened to be a qualified lawyer by training.

Their relationship had continued to improve and she was able to sift through the issues here and deal decisively with the identification and appointment of suitable judges for the Constitution courts after working with the Judge President.   Those jurors who the investigation revealed to have had "shady aspects of their appointment " revealed, were carefully approached and some voluntarily decided to step down in an attempt to salvage their reputation with a key focus on minimising the damage to the overall juristic governance of the country.

In any case, most of them, understood that they would lose what little respect that might still be out there for them in the public eye, and voluntarily took early retirement or resigned with little or no undue pressure placed on them.

Once this issue was attended to, Ms. Zungu had proved herself to have been a consummate professional and her reputation increased enormously in the country and especially among jurists everywhere.

Chapter 11:

The United Nations (UN) Visit

As part of routine meetings held at the UN, the came a time for Bheki as President of Mazania to represent his country by attending some key sessions there.   It was now winter in Mazania, his Presidential advisors had sat and explained some of the key initiatives and obligations that Mazania was expected to provide an update on.

Some of the financial, environmental and other global obligations the country had, were summarised and after some days of study, Bheki had agreed to meet with the expert advisory teams to obtain an update on what key items he had to provide an update on, as well as other duties he had to fulfill .

Previously   Bheki had not paid too much attention to the country's UN obligations, having spent most of his time focused on local priorities and issues that needed his attention.   After some days of watching briefing videos and reading up on various elements for his upcoming meetings at the UN in New York. He had grown sceptical and questioned how all these were good for Mazania, since he could not see much benefit to the country except obligations being imposed instead.

The further he read and gained an understanding, he could not help but come to resent how some countries at the UN were obviously more powerful than others based on their ability to veto some aspects they might not like. To him this amounted to nothing more than blatant double standards whichever way he looked at the issues.

Among various branches and sub-organisations focused on different focus areas, he could recognise the main ones as the General Assembly(UNGA), the United Nations Security Council(UNSC), the Economic and Social Council (UNESCO), the United Nations Trusteeship Council (this Council suspended operations in 1994), the International Court of Justice (ICC) and the UN Secretariat being the key ones.

Double Standards

Some Nations remained more equal than others, this had been one of Bheki's most poignant aspect that always stuck at the back of his mind whenever the thought of the nature and operations of the so called ' United Nations'. Also, even when he was a mere student studying for his initial Bachelor's degree, as he listened to some of the college debates he had attended, some thirty years earlier.

But now that he would have the opportunity as president to attend some meetings there in the near future.   He felt strongly that somewhere in those meetings and conferences , he would need to give a sincere view.

He also noted that his predecessors had barely touched on these aspect in their speeches.

Perceived and Real Undue Influence of some Countries over the UN.

For years it had been quietly observed that some countries were able to influence or push certain of their individual country's interest at the UN and in the process influence either policy or resolutions that came out of the UN.

This aspect of the UN was blatantly unfair and those who worked within the organisation and other states were aware of it but they could not do much about it given the " *unequal influence some countries wielded* ", since the five most powerful states with veto power often used this power to either bulldoze decisions or stand against the rest of the states who often, were in the majority but could be denied their motions because of the same Veto power.

The five permanent countries in the UNSC with veto power were :
- The United States of America
- The United Kingdom
- France
- China
- Russia

No Consequences on some Countries for Violation of UN Resolutions

In the past some UN member states had gone on their own in taking actions that often were against what was voted for at the UN, this had increasingly become apparent.   Oddly enough most of the traditional media reported minimally on this aspect. Often the dominant narrative carried by the media was one that served the government of their respective country.   This resulted in a rather misleading view of the UN as a fair organisation.

The were even cases of some countries going against UN resolutions already passed which if anything served to send an indirect signal as to

the effectiveness or lack thereof of the UN to
some extent.

Key examples that had taken place in more
recent times, included:

A. Israel / Palestine :(Resolution nr. 2334).
Resolution 2334 called for an end to Israeli
settlement building in December 2016   These
two nations had continued to live next to each
other in a state of low levels of animosity for
over 2 decade,   some efforts had been made
to find a peaceful resolution by having a two
state solution in the early 2000's but as the
years went on the situation had worsened with
more and more territory being taken despite the
resolution of the UN which had called for an
end to settlement building.

B. Bombing of Libya :- (Resolution UNSCR
1973).   This resolution empowered national
governments acting alone or through regional
organisations to take all necessary measures to
protect civilians and enforce a no-fly zone over
Libya.
In this instance, the US, France had gone on
missions to bomb and depose the leader of this
country against the express resolution given by
the UN. With the end result that the country
ended up being plunged into a dire and worse

condition than when it was before their unsanctioned military action.

C. America / Iraq War (Resolution 1441 (2002))
Similarly as the world had come to discover , the initial justification for the invasion and destruction was based on lies of the WMD (Weapons of Mass Destruction). From a UN resolution's perspective the resolution did not support the invasion and removal of the government of S.Hussein.

After attending various sessions and meeting different Presidents of other countries , a week later he returned home having some insights to better prepare for his first address or speech, scheduled for some four months later.

Chapter 12:

Organisation for Regional Unity Priorities

It was at one of the regular regional conferences of the countries bordering Mazania that Bheki was attending when several questions were posed to Bheki related to some of his views on the regional body.   The questions posed were not so much about his country but more about the region as a whole, up to this point he had made a point not to criticise his neighbouring governments and generally remained neutral as far as far as he could.

While he listened to the various heads of state give their updates and highlighting their priority areas , he could not help but note that various speakers had some differences in what they saw as their country's priority areas as leaders of the region.

As part of ongoing and regular regional meetings that Mazania was a part of, Bheki had attended several of these meeting at a senior level as Governor before becoming President.

Several objectives were being pursued as part of the priorities for Regional economic, security and good neighborliness.

The prime objective of the regional body was ultimately to improve trade, industry and ultimately jobs and quality of life for all its their respective citizens preferably without having a negative on impact on the citizen of neighbouring countries.

The areas of prime focus were :

A. Economy - Inter-Country Trade Infrastructure:

The Primary need that is common among the countries in the region related to how best to improve productivity for the region with regard to Infrastructure needed for trade,in transporting goods amongst the members states.

<u>Ports, Rail and Roads</u> :   It had been acknowledged that efficiencies in these areas needed improving and projects had been established to improve on this over a period of time

<u>Job Creation</u>:   Given that one of each country's priorities had been in one or other way linked to the improvement of the economy with the aim of creating jobs, which in turn increased each country's income levels and indirectly contributed to the fiscus which usually in turn increased tax revenues and pleased the voters, job creation was one of the main election

cries from across the region.   It is in part for this
reason the economy's improvement was intrinsically
linked to the overall improvement of jobs generated in
each country.

B. Currency :

Discussions with regard to why they still found
themselves having to trade based on a currency that
was foreign to their shores , namely the US Dollar .

C. Unfair trade practices :

In the region the proliferation of grey imports, such as
in cigarettes and inferior quality products were often
dumped on the country often resulting in a negative
impact on their country's competitiveness of their
respective countries.

This often resulted in job losses and general negative
impact on their economies.   It had been observed
that often the same countries dumping such products
and services, would themselves not tolerate other
countries doing the same in their countries.

D. Porous Borders and Visa Management:

Often the impact of undocumented entry of people
fleeing problems in their own countries, either as

economic or political refugees in their own countries needed to be better controlled, since it had often been used as a ruse for other personal reasons. Unfortunately this often meant one country's meagre resources often being usurped both non-citizens and as a consequent end up having to negate the impact on the host countries social objectives in most cases.

Terrorist acts following poor border control:
Given sporadic and often unforeseen acts of terror from religious and other fringe groups, it had been agreed.

E. Safety and Security (Law Enforcement):

As part of ensuring ongoing safety and security for their citizens, the member states had agreed to good neighbourliness and joining hands when faced with common threats, some of these included:

F. Foreign Power presence and Influence:

Most notable was to balance Army base presence from entities outside of the continent.   Given that African Governments had no foreign bases anywhere in the world, it had finally been acknowledged that the present of foreign armies could be at some point be used against their country or neighbours interested, especially given the unfortunate history of colonisation in their region.

Differences in Priorities & Timelines !
Following Bheki taking note of the different priority areas each leader had touched upon.   He had decided to probe further on just how uniform the region's leaders were when it came to him addressing the gathering. Of all 4 countries, it was striking that despite priority areas being agreed upon, very few of the leaders addressed these in any notable way.

As a new leader amongst these brother countries, he resolved to put serious questions to the effectiveness of not driving the priorities they claimed to have.

G. Peer Review Mechanism with Teeth

The regional body had had a Peer Review Mechanism that they had agreed to some 5 years earlier.   Surprisingly though non of the principles they had adopted and agreed to were anywhere to be seen on the documents.

Having recently studied these, Bheki had noted that some of the principles agreed and enshrined in the agreements, some violations by the leaders were clearly in evidence. Most of these were largely based on the priorities they had agreed on. Key Priorities which had been agreed to related to Proceeds of Crime and Job creation .

Chapter 13:

Foreign Interference and Posturing

Returning from the Regional Summit, as if Bheki was not aware of just how open the leaders had been about how they were treated by the so called Foreign Partners, he could still not believe how much foreign interference they were compelled to put up with.

This was often done as a result of threats of reduction in investment, withdrawal of Donor funds and the like.   Settling down next to his loving wife, Loki, Bheki looked at his wife with a blank stare, after enjoying his favourite dish that his wife had prepared.

" *Love, are you alright ?.*" Loki enquired.   Bheki looking at Loki, appeared as a man who was clearly lost in his mind, almost as if waking up from a dazed dream, he muttered.   " *I'm ok sthandwa, I just can't believe some of the things that were mentioned in confidence with some of our regional leaders.*"

" *What things ?* " Loki demanded to know.   Taking a deep breath Bheki continued: "*I learned this week that most of the regional leaders secretly felt they had no choice and were systematically being forced to implement foreign investors interest , in some cases against what they themselves really believed in."* he said with a sigh of disbelief.

"But love, they are sovereign states, why can't they stand against them if they are not in full agreement with these foreign investors ?" Loki asked with interest.

" Well, its a bit complicated than that ..." Bheki sighed as he drank the remains of the contents of the glass of water sitting next to him. *" Simply put ,Sthandwa, Bababambe ngamancane ..."*,concluded Bheki.

"Mmm,   You mean they've got them by the short and curlies ....?" .she asked,   *" Exactly right, by the financial strings that are attached, that is, in the form of grants, loans, investments and the like "* concluded Bheki as he poured himself a full glass of fresh milk while Loki stared at him.

She recalled how at her economics conference, a few months earlier, several of the World Bank and IMF speakers had continued to talk about various qualification criteria, which often insisted on how African governments and others had to accept criteria that dictated how grants, loans, infrastructure and health practices needed to be adapted in order to meet certain national education and health priorities of the IMF or world bank, while ignoring the countries who had applied for the same loans.

She had wondered why it was that financial loans would be dependent on the adoption of certain population control measures as well as certain freedoms related to gender standards and enforcement by the governments applying for the loans.

This aspect had stuck out for her since most financial loans and grants from commercial banks hardly if ever had conditions related to Health, Education for Farming practices and so on by sovereign states.

Now with Loki lost in her own thoughts and not aware that Bheki was handing her a glass of her favourite Berries Juice, she was suddenly called back to reality as Bheki inquired.   " Ko - ko, anybody home …?"

Coming back from her thoughts she regained her composure and exhaled quietly, before continuing: "Now, I'm beginning to understand why they had those strange conditions in that conference.", she began explaining "Many of our Farming co-ops and ministry of agriculture officials had talked about such conditions but I never fully grasped just how insidious some of those financial investments had been."

" Its time, *Sthandwa* …." whispered Bheki as he handed her her favourite pair of shades, so that they might go to the beach for their Sunday afternoon walk .

" Ready for your Ice Cream , *Sthandwa* " Bheki asked with a big smile

" *Yebo, masihambe* ", Loki responded, it had been a long day, it was a Sunday, they had returned from Mass and had enjoyed their Lunch but had almost completely forgotten about their Sunday afternoon beach walk that they had agreed to have in the late afternoon as the cool breeze began to blow outside.

Although the kids were not around this week to accompany them, they had made a habit of going for their Sunday walk at the beach or in the nearby forest park as a way of connecting with nature and with each other.

They had kept the habit of going out as often as possible in order to ensure that their relationship and private life was not entirely forgotten about . They had entered into this political life as a married couple and a family, they were determined to ensure that when all was said and done their private family life would not suffer or be taken over by the demands of political work as it is often happens and could put a strain on their family life.

Bheki always looked forward to these occasions as they helped him to relax but also because they helped him to stay connected to real life.

Their body guards and minders knew of these rendezvous and wear sworn to keeping them secret at all costs.   Honestly, it was a rare occasion to see their employers behaving like regular people in this form, since their lives were often taken up with duties of office, rushing from one meeting to the next and usually impeccably dressed.   To see them all relaxed helped to remind the minders also to cultivate their own private family relationships.

Chapter 14:

Jobs, Jobs, Jobs !

Its interesting that most of the preceding four administrations since the dawn of free and fair elections had come to office promising Job creation amongst other things.

The electorate, desperate for jobs had repeatedly bought into this aspect of the electoral promise only to receive inadequate jobs created compared to the number of unemployed in Mazania.

If anything the situation had continued to worsen as politicians of various municipalities, State and National governments appeared to pay lip service to this aspect.   Some jobs were created, however these paled poorly compared to the amount of effort or investment made elsewhere.

It almost seemed as if the governments had forgotten the prime deliverable of most governments , namely:

- Infrastructure - Water, Sanitation , Water and Roads
- Job Creation

- Safety and Security(Policing, Border Management)
- Education and Health Services..
- Laws, Regulation, Policies to support all of the above.

Of all of these basic but essential services provided by most governments, Job creation has and remains one of the key ratings that voters often focus on . This reality is quite understandable because without jobs people are not able to earn a living to support themselves and their loved ones especially.   Given that often citizens also have to pay towards the education of their children and for their health services.   Jobs naturally received a higher priority from the electorate's point of view.

So, when governments fail to provide Jobs then they fail to:

- Provide Reliable Water, Road Infrastructure,Reliable and affordable Electricity, they indirectly are failing to provide Jobs since these services are form the basics for job creation.

Cost and Perks of Government Employees :
Recognising this fact, Bheki had long recognised that in addition to the infrastructure requirements, one of his career ambitions was to improve the efficiencies of available financial resources in the country, which

was why as Mayor and later as State Governor he had focused on reducing lavish perks and expenses for officials.   Now as President he had not lost sight of the need for reasonable cost of the state employees versus the needs of the rest of the citizens, who often had no job to speak of.

Vacancies in Department positions ;
He continued to challenge his ministers to provide monthly reports on what they were doing to meet their primary goals and objectives, while making sure that available jobs were either filled urgently or steps taken to fast track graduates or Matriculants who could fill those jobs.

Sadly, in previous administrations this aspect of unfilled positions was not given adequate attention with the result that the return of approved budgets to the fiscus had become normal, because some of the departments were not spending their allocated budgets due to capacity or poor management in one form or other.   Working closely with his deputy President, Ms. Zungu, they were bent on making sure that this aspect of job creation would be adequately addressed.

This was relatively easy for the presidential team to work on this aspect since they were both very passionate about addressing the Job creation challenge in their country.

Private Business Preference for Foreign vs. Local Staff :

The other gapingly obvious aspect that contributed to the poor job creation situation, was the ease with which private industry had been allowed to higher foreigners instead of locals, since they demanded lower wages, often with this practice resulting in local of Mazanians, either losing-out or not being given priority when hiring.

In line with most country's common practice, Bheki insisted that employers prioritise the hiring of Mazanians without dual citizenship.   Employees were now required to give a motivation with clear evidence before a foreign national could be hired, instead of a local citizen.

Chapter 15:

Cabinet Review !

Every quarter Bheki, being the hands on manager he had always been, had insisted on meeting with his Departmental ministers at least once.   This was in addition to the monthly reports they were charged to provide.   In addition to this reports were requested when the were key areas of concern that arose on an ad hoc basis.

The Auditor General, facilitated the collation and verification of all the reports, although the summary and update had to be sent to the President directly by the relevant minister or head of the department without exception.

This was designed to ensure that the political leadership of the department and the administrative details shared were also clear to the political leader as well.   So, the minister could not just merely delegate the report to a junior person since he or she had to defend the report in the event of questions coming from the President.

The Cabinet had become aware that this monthly report for which the President had made clear to them that it would be used as the prime written update they and their performance would be evaluated based on its accuracy, professionalism and details it captured.

It had been almost 10 months since the new Cabinet or administration had been using this method when Bheki met with the cabinet ministers, he would ask probing questions on progress and track issues they highlighted therein.

So, in his one-on-ones the ministers had become acutely aware that this monthly report would form the basis for most if not all performance matrix that was used to measure their performance.

After about two quarters , Bheki and his deputy president had started to highlight ministries that were performing above target, those performing well as well as ministries that would need corrective action to be taken , either by supporting the relevant political figurehead or replacing them.

Faced with the areas that needed intervention Bheki was faced with having to effect a cabinet reshuffle.

He subsequently met with the political party president, Ms. Zungu , since he was by arrangement the party deputy President but President of the Government or Cabinet, and explored possibilities of what could be done with the ministries and their respective political heads who had underperformed.

After some initial discussion, Ms. Zungu and Bheki, eventually agreed on how the cabinet reshuffle could be handled.

They had to reach an agreement in order to ensure a cohesive and cooperative party executive as well as the country's Cabinet.

After several meetings they agreed that they would effect the cabinet reshuffle after a full year of the new administration

Chapter 16:

Performance Agreements &
Consequences !

Following the Performance Agreements the cabinet
ministers had accepted at the time of their
appointment, it was time for repercussions and
consequences.

After the 3rd quarter, Bheki working close with his
deputy President, had met with each individual
Cabinet minister and where necessary, gave the final
warning to correct or improve on the areas of concern
in the following quarter.   The President and his
deputy had given them clear areas of concern and
warned them that a lack of improvement would force
his hand if no improvement was forthcoming.

He made it clear as to what improvement metric was
needed to avoid misunderstanding but also in order
to give them a fair chance at improving.

The Departments or Ministries he was concerned
with the most were Agriculture, Water ,Small
Business and Labour.   He argued that if these

departments improved their performance this would have a significant positive impact on the country's job situation.

The well performing ministries included Foreign Relations, Mining and Forestry.   The real superstar performers were the Ministries of Health and Education.

This was largely boosted by the campaign promise of having all state employees use state Health and Education facilities instead of private ones whenever possible.

This meant that because the poor performing ministries were now under pressure to improve quality of service and efficiency.

The departments that improved enormously had done so because senior officials themselves had to use the facilities for their own families and for themselves with the ultimate result that corrective action was taken speedily and the overall mindset of quickly running to private institutions had been curtailed by the sheer will of political policy and selfish reasons, on the part of the officials in charge.

Although the Cabinet minsters involved had taken a lot of strain and initial criticism after coming to office, after a relatively short time of taking over the

ministries, they had been transformed into superstars
of the cabinet given the amount of positive change
they had managed to bring during their time in office.

Things were not perfect, but overall regular feedback
from news journalists , teachers, students and
parents had increasingly become positive and public
opinion had begun to laud them for their efforts.

Chapter 17 :

Not so United Nations

Double Standards

" Some Nations remained more equal than others within the United Nations" , this was a cry that had continued to be heard with the voices getting louder since the founding of the UN.   Although the structure of the UN was based on the outcomes of the Second World War, the war had been over for more than seven decades, however there seemed to be no serious intention to correct this anytime soon.

At various UN forums different National representatives had voiced their displeasure at this unequal reality, only to be ignored entirely or various excuses were peddled along with non of the five nations with veto power , hardly ever adequately responding to the voices of discontent in any significant way.

United Nations Security Council (UNSC)

This same unfair allocation of votes within UNSC remained unchanged.   Those who have a favored voting position being unwilling or resistant to any changes proposed by nations who are in an unfavorable, non-veto but majority position

Change or Leave

While many Nations saw the value of being in one global entity and being able to cooperate with the rest of the UN family, often Nations felt that they should try to change the status quo or leave the organisation.   However, because the is no other global entity of the same type, many nations chose to remain as part of the organisation albeit begrudgingly in some cases.

So, as Bheki was preparing for his maiden speech , these were some of the things he found himself pondering.

Globalist Agenda, NGO

Given that the UN had various sub-groups focused on humanitarian areas for health, Poverty eradication, security and the like.   It had become increasingly apparent that some of the Powerful Nations had started to use some of these organisations to pursue their own nationalistic agendas.

This was bound to happen given that most of the staffers of these organisation by default or perhaps design tended to come predominantly from so called Western countries.

Preparation for the UN Speech.

After some months of preparation, the time eventually came for Bheki to make his way to New York for his address.   A week before he left Mazania, he insisted on having a special session of the cabinet, so as to confirm from them some issues and to take their input into consideration.

 In this meeting he asked for key points only, to consider or incorporate in his address at the UN.   In this meeting in attendance was the country's permanent representative at the UN as well as the Minister of Foreign Affairs.

Some of the points the cabinet ministers asked him to include,were :

- **Dept. Of Health** = Better Control on the costs of medicine with regard to Provisioning of Stock vs. Profit. (i.e. Original vs Generic medicines)

- **Dept. of Education** = Global Standardisation of Tertiary qualifications

- **Dept.of Defence** = a Seat in the UNSC and Better Respect and Implementation of Resolutions passed by the UNSC.
- **Dept. of Agriculture** = Private vs. Public interest guardianship over GMO (Generically Modified Organisms) Seeds
-

Chapter 18 :

The Inaugural UN Speech

It had been a long flight, on arrival both Bheki and his presidential advisor, Loki were exhausted.   They had arrived a few days early, enough time for them to take a tour of the city before getting down to business.

They had asked for their trip to set aside at least two days of no formal meetings so they could use the time to spend some time together.   It had been a long year and both of them had missed out on quiet time together.

They had arrived in the evening and had dinner quietly in their suite and had an early night.   The next morning they attended a few business meetings that were scheduled but not announced to the press and were held in private.

In the afternoon they went for a formal Dinner at Mazania's Ambassador's residence where they met for the first time the full Staff of the consulate and took various questions the officials presented.   It was a good evening and they even managed to indulge in private conversation in their native language while enjoying traditional home cooking which they had not expected to find in New York.

It was a jovial evening with most of the permanent staff who had not met their president in attendance. Loki managed to even get the inside scoop on the who's who of the lady influencers at the UN as well as   to what fashion and styles were in or out.   This in turn gave her some tips on how best to choose her style.

A bit awkward though, was the fact that here they had to put up with some crazy weather and the snow had blanketed most if not all of the city and its surroundings.

After a full day of working in the Ambassador's office for a full day, Bheki had had enough time as he read his speech to his most trusted sceptic and partner Loki.

Loki had raised an eyebrow after seeing and hearing some of the points Bheki had penned and raised some questions.   Some heated but respectful exchanges took place.   By this time they had come to understand each other so well, that often they could read each other's minds without the other needing to provide the details.

This dynamic was the one aspect of their relationship they valued most in each other and were always aware of just how blessed they actually were since they could do this almost instinctively on most occasions.

While Bheki was working , Loki had gone to spend some time with the Ambassador's wife.   On her return she had shared with Bheki some of what she had learnt.

The following day would be the day of the Speech. Although Bheki had become accustomed to giving speeches, somehow on this occasion facing what would be the prime of the world's leaders, somehow he felt himself a little ill-prepared.

The morning arrived, the couple travelled to the UN Building they had visited two days earlier, but this time they were no mere guests but would be part of its working machinery since Bheki would be giving a formal address.   One aspect that made an impression on him was just how bureaucratic the organisation was, so much so that he had begun to wonder if the bureaucracy was of benefit overall or if the bureaucracy had become an impediment instead.

Then the hour came as Bheki was given the place to sit while waiting his turn to address the house.   Loki like the traditional wife she had always been was

seen holding his arm as a show of support, this was
an important step in their life as a couple and not just
as representatives of Mazania, also how far their
journey had brought them.   All those many years
ago, when they had attended a mere mayoral
address in their small semi rural town where they
lived.

Looking at her husband of some 21 years, Loki gave
her husband a loving Kiss, as he got up and walked
to the Speaker's booth to address the house and
Began :

" *Ladies and Gentlemen, Good afternoon, I greet you
in the name of the people of Mazania.   I would like
to premise my address with a question if I May ….
We call ourselves the United Nations, but …*".   Bheki
paused as he took a long look around the house for a
few seconds .

 "*Are we United ?* " as he glanced around, almost as
if he was waiting for a response to his rhetorical
question, he then continued :

" *On behalf of my people , which I have the privilege
to represent, I'd like to highlight a few points and
issues that my people continue to ask* ".   He glanced
at Loki who smiled almost as a gesture of offering
him support.

" Given the short time I have to speak here, I will not re-iterate the same feel good, known positions that my predecessors have endorsed and that I also endorse with regard to democracy, governance, fairness and equality that this house and I agree upon. .."

" Instead I am going to focus on the concerns that need our joint attention to resolve and preferably resolve urgently if this house is to remain of relevance to the world and hopefully turn the direction or perception of being a talk-shop, with no ability to effectively enforce fairness and resolutions that the house and its organs passes,and then watches on the sidelines as they get ignored or sidelined by one or some of its very own member states, with impunity

.

Some like myself have come to believe that its preferable that there be a transition to an entity were no special treatment for any one or few nations as currently enjoyed by those five nations that enjoy unique veto power to reverse, stall or block any resolutions passed by over 190 member countries this house passes, especially in the UNSC.

The unfortunate reality is that often the is no logical justification being given for such vetoing of the democratic votes offered, yet we as the United Nations, pretend to the rest of the world that this house is Democratic in its decision making, yet we carry on as if this is normal , such hypocrisy is unsustainable, perhaps its time we, ourselves led by example, don't you Agree ?, or are we saying that some are more equal than others ? "

Pausing for effect once more, and with both his hands turned up and with a smirk on his face , he continued and asked

" … given that many of you have been in this house for many years, longer than I have, do I really need to continue ? "   Once more he paused and glanced into the faces of the 5 countries's representatives.

At this stage everyone knew exactly which countries he was referring to, some individuals members in the assembly clapped their hand, these were various country representatives who have over time highlighted this very fact he was talking about, he then proceeded:

" For the purposes of numerating some of these and in order to enable some hopeful form of overdue but obvious response that is necessary here, lets have a look at some of these : "

With the General Assembly now having gone so quiet, one could hear a pin drop and with increased attention from most of the nation's representatives, he shuffled his notes and then said.

" I note that I have only a few minutes left, so here's the list, feel free to reach out to our UN Ambassador, Mr. Zitha, should a detailed list be required, some of these key areas are :

- **Health** = Better Control on medicine costs with regard to Health vs. Profit.

The overt real and perceived manner in which prices are set in a way to maximise profits at the expense of our people's lives cannot continue as it is, this is unacceptable.   We need to change the laws so that copyright restrictions and limits for time to produce generic medicines in a much-shorter time, so more lives can be saved.   At the risk of stating what should be obvious, medicines are for saving lives not for profit.

- **Education and Training** = Global Standardisation of Tertiary qualifications

- **Defence** = a Seat in the UNSC for each continent or region, at least and Compulsory Respect of UN Resolutions passed by the UNSC, with real consequences for those states who deliberately go against such resolutions that have been properly voted for.   The fact that Africa constitutes one of the biggest voting blocks and yet has no vote in the UNSC remains a travesty.

" … and Perhaps a simple question, 50 years after World War II ended, the same War for which many of our men were killed in the name of doing the right thing and contributing to fairness in the world, why do some nations continue to be more equal than others when all our people similarly gave their lives for the same freedoms as those from the nations with veto power ? ".   Bheki asked rhetorically, he then continued :

"... or are we condoning and Affirming that might is right ?, the more nuclear heads a nation has, the more they deserve to have a seat at the UNSC, is this Really what we are saying ? "

- **Agriculture** = Private vs. Public interest guardianship over GMO (Genetically Modified Organisms) Seeds

" How do we justify the pushing out of age old farming methods and farmers so that some global companies can profiteer at the expense of citizens and future seed-independence, the basis for any societies food security ? and finally he concluded :

- ___Genuine Sovereignity___ = *Not some tainted with invisible provisos from the so called UN bodies or financial institutions dominated by the same 5 nations with Veto power.   The same veto power that is surreptitiously extended in these same organisations for their selfish individual country's priorities at the expense of the rest of humanity.*

With his time up, Bheki thanked the assembly and proceeded to his seat.   Following his speech, the news media, especially the independent online media covered and held various debates on his speech, some in favour and some criticising him for one or other thing, however not many could ignore his frank and honest truths he had highlighted.

In the evening after the business of the day at the UN had been concluded, the Mazanian ambassador and staff through an unexpected cultural evening in appreciation of their President's inaugural visit and speech at the UN, which was greatly appreciated by the Presidential couple.

Loki, although initially unhappy with the speech during Bheki's rehearsal, could not be prouder of her husband's unorthodox but heartfelt delivery of his maiden speech and the overwhelmingly positive response it received.

The loving couple landed safely back in Mazania to a
heroes welcome.   Even his ardent critics could not
contain themselves in the first parliamentary seating,
heaping unexpected words of support and
appreciation.

THE END.

" There is no passion to be found playing small in settling for a life that is less than the one you are capable of living "

~ N.H.Mandela